# PREFACE

This exposé introduces and describes the background of the members of Engine 21. Engine 21 was Chicago's first organized paid African American Firefighting Company. The writer provides information and insight on changes from Slavery to Freedom in the African American Community and the political impact that affected change for African American Firefighters, during this period of reconstruction in America.

Most people are unaware that the concept and use of the fire house sliding pole was invented and made popular, in Chicago and nationally, by the foreman and members of Engine 21. The fire house sliding pole assisted in the accomplishment of practicing fast run-outs when responding to assimilated day drill alarms of 12-15 seconds and at night drill alarms of 25-30 seconds. In 1888, a report from the Chicago Daily Tribune indicated the assimilated drill alarms helped Engine 21 to become the first arrival at many alarms and fires; thereby, validating the use of the fire pole. Furthermore, Engine 21 led Chicago's fire companies in fire runs, fire work time and total runs, and stimulated competition among fire companies. From 1872-1927, Engine 21 participated in most, if not all, major fires that occurred in Chicago's Downtown area, namely, the Iroquois Theater fire December 30, 1903 and many other fires in Printers Row.

It is my opinion that none of this would be possible without the tenacity, foresight, and heroic efforts of Mayor Joseph Medill (1823-1899). Mayor Medill was a lawyer, abolitionist, newspaper publisher and advisor to President Abraham Lincoln during the Civil War and he was the Mayor of Chicago from 1871-1873. In 1872, Mayor Medill helped John Jones get elected as Chicago's first Cook County Commissioner. Additionally, he hired the first "plain clothes" police officer and established Engine 21 as America's first organized, paid fire company. Mayor Medill was not only a great American, but a bona fide hero and visionary. The book: *Black Heroes of Fire,* best describes this group of brave and courageous men.

# ONE

## BLACK HEROES OF FIRE

1873 Engine 21 Uniform Inspection, *Allen Williams Collection*

Today, firefighting and Emergency Medical Services (EMS) are America's vanguard to our society in times of need. In the event of floods, fires, earthquakes, train wrecks, airplane crashes and other disasters, the Fire Service is America's first line of defense. The Fire Service, in many communities across America, is extremely under-represented by those that live and pay taxes in their own communities. Many have been locked out of the Fire Services profession in Northern cities, dating back to its inception during the volunteer days of the 18th and 19th Centuries in America, *i.e. 1818, African Firefighter's Association of Philadelphia.*

Race and Firefighting in Antebellum South – Municipalities of the 1700 and 1800 (authored by, Lykee B. Davis) purports the need to provide fire protection in order to prevent the fires that could destroy cities. *Dennis Smith's History of Firefighting in America: 300 years of Courage, (Smith 1980)* illustrates the threat posed by fire to urban environments of the period and how fire departments in the North and South developed. Antebellum South Carolina and Georgia dealt with this threat by adopting the fire protection policies of New York, Philadelphia, and other Northern counterparts in the use of slave and free Black firefighters.

Black Firefighters from Charleston and Savannah, 1850's,
*J Paul Getty Museum and Robert W. Woodriff library*

The differences in the demographic makeup and character of these northern fire departments reflected differences in urban societies of the South and North. Southern cities allowed for and encouraged the use of African Americans in their fire departments out of necessity, Slaves and free Black men made up a significant portion of the fire department in Charleston, Macon and Savannah. These departments were comparable to their northern counterparts in equipment, but the absence of adequate manpower could not save a city. Without the manpower provided by Black firefighters, the safety of these cities would have been in jeopardy.

Northern fire companies were a part of an urban world that was exclusively male and most likely white. In Philadelphia, Blacks did not seem to have joined the private fire companies and when they tried to form their own African Fire Association in 1818, the hostility of white fire companies thwarted their attempt. In the North, the civic nature of the fire departments led to attempts to ban Black men.

New Orleans hired its first Black firefighter in 1817. Seven years later, Blacks were fighting fires in Savannah, Columbia (1840) and Richmond (1864). Charleston was documented as paying whites more than Blacks for their service, and unlike Blacks, whites received a fine instead of a whipping if they failed to appear at the cry of "FIRE". In 1821, about seventy-five free Blacks formed the *Franklin Fire Engine and Hose Company*, thus Blacks composed a majority of local firefighters until the mid-1870's.

The Savannah Fire company was established in 1824 by order of the general assembly. In 1825, Savannah's city council passed an ordinance to count the free Blacks and Slaves who were firefighters, those who did not respond could be fined, jailed or whipped. In 1828, the department consisted of 178 slaves, 96 free Black men and 17 whites of the Oglethorpe Company. In 1857, the Black fire companies in the department were the *Axe Hook & Ladder Company* which had 53 firefighters; the hose company #2 which had 23 - both stationed at Fireman's Hall; and Engine Company #4 which had 65 and was stationed in Wright Square. While the Black fire companies were manned by free Blacks who did the manual labor, they were supervised and commanded by white officers. Black men like other firefighters were paid if they were first to sound an alarm or put water on the fire.

Fire protection was a necessity for urban environments of the 18th and 19th centuries and without the protection provided by the service, a city could be reduced to ashes. In Savannah, the Black firemen made up the majority of the fire department. *Fire of Liberty* argues that the use of Blacks in the Charleston Fire Department resulted from the need for man-power. Without the support of the Black population, Charleston, Macon and Savannah would not have been able to survive the perils of fire that the urban centers faced. The need for Blacks to serve in 1842 required Blacks between the ages of 18 and 42 to serve. In post Antebellum period, Southern fire departments more radically aligned with northern fire departments. The Jim Crow system brought "White Only" fire departments into being in Charleston, Macon and Savannah.

# TWO

## ENGINE 21, CHICAGO'S
## FIRST BLACK FIRE COMPANY

Black Engineer racing to a fire on a steam engine
Allen Williams photo collection

Scholar Amber Bailey described Engine 21 as "an experiment with interracial democracy in an era of reconstruction, 1872-1927." Engine 21 stood at the vanguard to Chicago's local reconstruction. The story of Engine 21 is the story of reconstruction in Chicago and America.

It was a period in history, when federal and congressional reconstruction was initiated with Marshall Law, control in the South and government overhaul in the North. All, to redefine the meaning of the United States Constitution and the real meaning of democracy, has always been short-lived. Another phase of institutional racism was not far off.

As Amber stated, "The federal government failed to enforce and protect many of the congressional and legislative victims' achievements during and following the federal reconstruction period."

We cannot talk about the establishment of Engine 21 as a fire company without painting a bigger picture of the life and times of that period, such as: Congressional laws, state and local ordinances created during this era and the institutional racism that followed. Currier & Ives' creation, illustration and publication of the Dark Town Fire Brigade is a classic illustration of the defamation and libel of Black firefighters, then and now. Lithograph caricatures such as slightly demoralized firefighters on parade are examples of numerous postcard-type photos of Black men portrayed as bumbling idiots and misfits.

19ᵗʰ century Darktown fire brigade – by Currier & Ives publishers

Ironically, only two Black organized fire companies existed when these graphic demoralizing illustrations were created, Engine 21 and Hose co. #9 of Indianapolis, Indiana; thus, affecting the hiring, maintenance and promoting of Black firefighters in America until well after WW II. Blacks were portrayed through negative stereotyped images, such as firefighters acting mentally slow, illustrating them as being physically grotesque and morally inept; thus, injuring and reinforcing a false premise of Black men and Black firefighters.

For over 100 years, these images have represented the racial attitudes of Whites who sought to keep Blacks out of the fire service. Currier and Ives' false image and negative stereotypes of Black men re-enforced the fears of whites regarding Black firefighters. Nationally, Black men were not hired as firefighters in America until well after World War II; and this has stymied Blacks' ability to get employment and promotions in the fire service, in general. Black men, such as Thomas J. Martin, the inventor of the fire extinguisher in 1872; Garrett A. Morgan, the inventor of the gas mask in 1914; and Engine 21's invention of the firehouse sliding pole discredit these negative stereotypes of Black men and Black firefighters.

Laws and ordinances created between1865 to 1877, were constructed to aid Blacks during this transitional period from slavery to freedom. In Chicago, the transition began in 1865 with the repeal of Black laws. These laws were established to grant Blacks their freedom, their right to vote, their right to equal treatment at public facilities, and the right to equal employment. Furthermore, desegregation of the public-school system allowed Blacks the opportunity to attend school. However, these laws were ineffective because they were not enforced.

Mayor Joseph Medill was Chicago's catalyst for change and was determined to bring Blacks into Chicago's mainstream. Medill a reformist mayor, spearheaded Chicago's Black reconstruction, following the Great Chicago Fire of October 1871. This was accomplished by taking control over the economic and social affairs, as well as the city's police and fire boards, who were adamant against hiring Blacks in city government. Medill declared the Colored man has the same rights to suffrage as the white man. He earned a reputation as a champion of civil rights for the Negroes and was most responsible for Chicago's reconstruction. He went on to help establish Blacks as policemen, firefighters and politicians.

Engine 21

Engine 21, Foreman David B. Kenyon (far right), *Property of Fred Olney,*

Their first apparatus was a steamer called the Vigilant which was considered a first-class pumper built by *Amoskeog Manufacturing Company* from Manchester, New Hampshire.

Also, occupied in Engine 21 was a two-wheel hose cart drawn by two horses. These members lived in the fire houses and went home occasionally to visit. It was not until the early 1900's did Chicago establish a second shift giving their members one day of rest. The second shift added another 7 to 8 members per shift, increasing Chicago's members from 7 to 14. Engine 21's first fire house was originally located at 47 Eldridge Court, and was occupied in a rented warehouse of temporary quarters until a new fire house was built.

Chicago's Engine 21, the first organized paid Black fire company in the nation entered service December 21, 1872 with one foreman, David B. Kenyon, one assistant foreman, James E. Porter (first Black Lt.), Engineer Henry Pethybridge and 6 Black firemen. The pipe-men were Willie Hawkins and James Johnson, hose cart drivers were Steven Paine and George Adams, the watchman was George Reed and the stoker was William Watkins.

In December of 1875, Engine 21 relocated to 1213 S. Plymouth Court (313 Third Street). The first fire house was located originally between the wealthy homes of the rich, east of Wabash Ave. Poor Jewish, Irish, German, Polish and Blacks who lived west of State Street, stimulated questions of competency and controversy by white firefighters who suggested these Black men were taking their jobs.

# THREE

## CHICAGO'S RECONSTRUCTION ERA

Mayor Medill, *Newberry Library collection*

The Chicago Tribune reported Blacks were being rewarded for their help during and following the great fire of October 8, 1871 which lent legitimacy to their cause. However, without the committed efforts of Mayor Medill, all would have been for naught. Chicago, like other large urban areas of the North and the South, never bought into the plan of reconstruction for Blacks; but, rather as an opportunity to further their goals and aspirations benefiting from segregated institutional racism.

The Honorable Mayor Joseph Medill was responsible for establishing Engine 21 as a fire company. Mayor Medill wore many hats: attorney, newspaper publisher, abolitionist, friend to President Lincoln and Reformist Mayor of Chicago.

His primary goal was to help rebuild Chicago and incorporate African Americans citizens into Chicago's mainstream. He was instrumental in helping his friend, businessman and abolitionist John Jones, get elected as Chicago's first Cook County Commissioner.

Photo of retired Commissioner John Jones,
Chicago first Black Cook County commissioner.
He was an abolitionist, businessman and politician. *Vivian G. Harsh Collection-CPL*

Mayor Medill assigned Chicago's first Black Plain Clothes Police Officer and established Engine 21 as Chicago's first Black fire company, all in his first year as mayor.

This era was considered as a period of society's reconstruction, coupled with Chicago's rebuilding the police and fire departments that had a reputation for incompetency and graft; thus, stimulating engine 21's existence. Ironically, though *Currier & Ives*, according to Amber Bailey, "The pulse of the white community (between 1884-89) created the Dark Town Fire Brigade, minimizing Engine 21's manhood by creating doubt of their abilities as firefighters, regardless of their overwhelming accomplishments, such as: the invention of the sliding pole, earning a reputation of being first in at fires, and leading the fire department in response statistics."

Many, if not all, of Engine 21's Black members were ex-slaves and Civil War Veterans. Foreman David Kenyon was a Captain, the highest rank served in the war and he was said to have led a Black regiment of men, making him an ideal candidate to lead this brave group of men. Seven years prior to establishing Engine 21, the Civil War ended, banning Slavery; and thereby granting equal rights, voting rights and citizenship to Blacks.

This fire company represented a major pillar of progress in America, thus becoming the glimmer of hope for other cities such as Indianapolis, Indiana, with their first Black Fire Company in 1876; and Washington D.C., where Blacks were used as firefighters sporadically around the city in integrated fire companies. Cities like Philadelphia didn't realize its first black firefighter until 1886, Columbus, Ohio 1892 and New York 1898.

Fires in Chicago were common, but the first great fire of October 1871 opened the eyes of businessmen, insurance companies and citizens alike when half of the city burned to the ground and left Chicago razed, leveled, and, broke. Chicago, like most urban cities at that time, was made of wood. The homes, light poles, sidewalks, commercial buildings, hotels and fences were all constructed from wood.

Prior to becoming firefighters, Blacks after the Civil War were only hired as porters, barbers, coachmen, waiters and teamsters and other low paying jobs. Now as firefighters, they were enabled to provide a better lifestyle for themselves and their families and shed the image with which society had branded: cheap labor, lazy, and not very intelligent.

As stated by Bailey, *"The Currier & Ives Lithographs* comics created a vision of Black firefighters as misfits and bumbling idiots who questioned their masculinity as firefighters, and then as men, starting with degrading caricatures that were proven false by Engine 21's members. Their invention of the Sliding Pole and their persistence at besting their rivals at battling fires eventually won out."

Engine 21 had to outshine the competition if they were to survive as a fire company.

# FOUR

## THE GREAT FIRES

Chicago following the first great fire, *Newberry Library photo collection*

While this city brought questions concerning Chicago's building construction, there were promises of change, yet still wood was used to construct temporary housing. Following Chicago's second great fire on July 14, 1874, the Black and poor communities burned, and insurance companies required that a fire district be established where only fire resistive construction was accepted. Ten years later, Chicago began building high rise buildings in its business district.

Chicago's population continued to grow extremely fast. During its incorporation between March 1837 and 1870, its population grew from a few hundred to about 300,000 with 4,000 Black residents. By 1890, Chicago had grown to one million residents with 14,000 Blacks in 20 years. The first great fire destroyed most of Chicago north of 9th Street and was fueled by thousands of wood structures and shacks with strong south winds and no rain for months. The first Great Chicago Fire killed over 300 people causing millions of dollars in damage and leaving most of the city homeless and in peril.

Chicago's housing stock with plenty of wood homes. The 2nd great fire strictly outlawed the building of wood homes inside of Chicago's downtown area when every other one was of brick and concrete. Chicago then went into its high-rise building phase in the mid 1880's or so.
*Chicago Historical society*

In 1874, approximately 4,000 to 5,000 African Americans lived in and around the City of Chicago. Many were scattered throughout the city, including the Northside and Westside of the city. However, 1,000 or so Blacks lived in the central district (2nd ward), between State Street to the east and 4th Street to the west, Roosevelt Road to the south and Van Buren to the north.

Most people lived in the area where they worked because of transportation limitations. Maids usually lived in the maid's quarters of their employers. Coach drivers lived in coach houses, usually where the horses were stored in the rear, separate from the main house. Other Blacks found residency in other areas of the city because segregation policies had not been created at that point. Chicago's primary building construction was of wood with two and three-story structures of mixed occupancy butted next to one another and mixed with residential and commercial properties. These structures were a living time bomb, and then fire struck again.

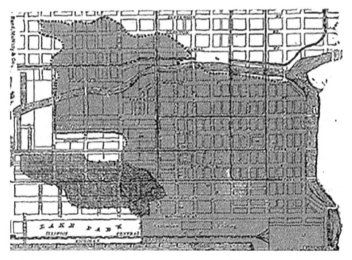

Map of Chicago conflagration fire, October 8th, 1871 and July 14, 1874.

The Black fire of July 14, 1874, the 2nd great Chicago fire, struck about 4:00pm on a Sunday afternoon. Engine 21 received an alarm for the corner of Roosevelt and Clark Streets. The Chicago *Daily Tribune* reported that Engine 21 was the first arriving fire company on the scene. The properties located at the addresses of 503 to 523 Clark Street were consumed by fire. This area of the city, which was spared by the first fire, was now under siege because of the large multitude of wood structures, shacks and shanties in this area.

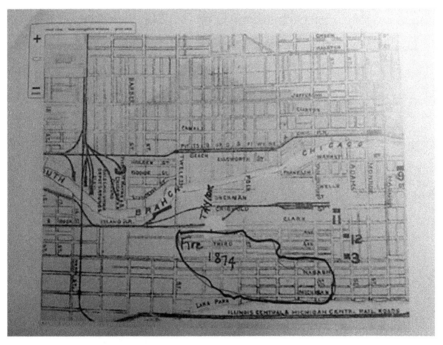

Layout of area affected by Chicago's second great fire – The Black Fire of July 14, 1874 which started Chicago's black migration to the south side.

This fire was reported to have started in a rag shop next door to an oil company, causing further complications. With a duplication of the weather conditions similar to the first great fire, southwest high winds, no rain, these tinder boxes went up like matchboxes. An explosion occurred at the rag shop, damaging Engine 21's apparatus and rendering it inoperable, and as reported by the *Chicago Tribune,* "killing a member of Engine 21 by the name of Williams." *(Records do not indicate a member by the name of Williams as being employed or suffering LODD).* A fire department in transition, inadequate water supply, and thousands of wood shacks assisted by high winds claimed everything in its path.

Olivet Baptist Church was destroyed during this inferno fire, along with other churches in the area. Quinn African Methodist Episcopal Church burned during the first Chicago Fire in 1871. The church did not find a permanent home until 1891 at 24$^{th}$ & Wabash. Quinn Chapel is historically considered as Chicago's first Black church followed by Olivet Baptist Church.

When this fire started, many parishioners were attending a picnic south of the city and the smoke could be seen for miles. After returning, from the picnic, the parishioners found their residences burned and leveled to the ground with all their belongings consumed by fire. The effects of this fire caused Blacks to start their migration up south State Street, seeking refuge from this catastrophic epoch well into the 1900's. The migration created the Black Belt and later, Bronzeville.

As reported by the Chicago Tribune and in the Chicago Fire Department annual reports, this fire consumed 47 acres of land (approximately 15 square blocks). Thirty citizens lost their lives, compared to 300 unfortunate souls reportedly lost in the first fire. This fire consumed 812 wooden structures, and 36 four to five-story brick structures of mixed occupancy, with businesses on the first floor and apartments and motels on the upper floors. The monetary loss of this fire totaled $3,845,000.00 in property damage with insurance companies paying out $2,200,000.00 in replacement costs. Only a small percentage of insurance claims were paid to Blacks because most could not afford insurance, which left them devastated and starting over, after losing everything.

Low wages and losing everything in this fire caused many hardships. Some Blacks boarded trains and relocated, and others set up temporary quarters until other means could be established. The winter of 1874 was reported to be extremely cold and bitter, bringing more hardships for these grieving families who were only nine years out of slavery. The area of the city that burned was referred to as Shanty Town and the notorious Cheyenne because of the red-light district they shared with ladies of the night, saloons, pick pockets, gamblers, thieves and the numerous wood shanties built there.

The second great fire was referred to as the *Black Fire*. The city and insurance companies created a fire district where the building of wood homes was strictly outlawed, causing the city to create the building department and the fire prevention bureau. In time, Chicago's water supply system improved with the replacement of wooden mains and underground cisterns which were strategically placed around the city when fire occurred, providing a greater supply of water. Fire Insurance patrols were created to salvage insurance carriers' property, keeping payouts down.

# FIVE

## CAPTAIN KENYON'S SLIDING POLE

Photo taken from the Political History of Chicago, 1837-1887, by M.L. Ahern In 1886. Photo promotes the sliding pole invented in Chicago.

The creation and concept of the Sliding Pole was invented at the 313 Third Ave. (1213 S. Plymouth Court) fire house - a three-story building where a fire lookout watch was usually manned on the top floor. Firefighter George Reed was said to have slid the first pole. The first Sliding Pole was a diagonal wooden pole, which was used to hoist hay to the 3$^{rd}$ floor where it was stored for horses. When an alarm was received, everyone took the stairs except Firefighter Reed who slid the pole. By the time the other members reached the main floor, he was asked how he got down so fast. He replied, "I slid the pole."

The first wood pole was originally made of 4 x 4-inch Georgia pine, the corners were cut off and sanded round to 3 inches. Shellac was applied with paraffin added to make it slippery. Foreman David Kenyon asked Chief Breenan for permission to cut holes in the floor. He agreed; but, if this idea did not work he was told they would have to replace the holes with their own money. By April 1878, the *Chicago Fire Department* annual report mentioned sliding poles were being installed in fire houses throughout the city. It was said that the Sliding Pole increased the firefighters' response times when responding to fires.

Captain David Kenyon – like Mayor Medill he was innovative, courageous and a true hero. He manned E-21 for a number of years and was given credit for inventing the fire house sliding pole. When responding to an alarm as acting Deputy Fire Marshall, after being thrown from his buggy, he was run over by Engine 32 and later died of his injuries. *Newberry Library, Chicago public library.*

The members of this fire company drilled regularly on sliding the pole and hooking up their horses to rapidly exit the door. When tested during the day, response times varied between 12-14 seconds, and at night 26-30 seconds. This fire company recorded at the top of

Chicago's list for responding to the most working fires, run time, and overall responses.

The concept of the Sliding Pole was ingenious, but the use of wood was discontinued after three years because of splinters and other maintenance problems. Splinters injured numerous firefighters, so in 1880 Boston patented the brass pole, taking this concept to the next level by replacing wood as a fire sliding pole. Furthermore, Foreman David Kenyon never received a patent for his invention. He was told to give the pole a purpose and a name, but never returned to secure his patented invention. Documentation verifies where this concept was originated and first conceived.

# SIX

## THE 19<sup>TH</sup> CENTURY

Expansion of the black community – Engine 19, located 3444 S. Rhodes Avenue, following their change of quarters from Engine 21, 47 W. Taylor Street in 1927.

In 1878, Engine 21 participated in a parade honoring President Rutherford G. Hayes. Engine 21 marched alongside more than one thousand Illinois soldiers and a company of Black soldiers. Most, if not all, of Engine 21's members were Civil War veterans, making this parade a "parade of heroes."

By 1881, Engine 21 was on the road again, relocating to 14 W. Taylor Street in the Rail Yard. The relocation removed Engine 21 from the public's eye. Responses to fire emergencies extended further and further south of downtown, following Chicago's Black Community. Many Black people who migrated from the South used the fire house for information and directions.

Engine 21's fire district contained every type of building construction and business, from large commercial mill constructed buildings to lumber yards and railroad yards with rail cars. Printer's row was a district where large amounts of printing with flammable inks and oils were prevalent. Three and four-story apartment structures, and some mixed occupancies with businesses, such as hardware stores on the first floor, were included in Engine 21's boundaries (lake Front to the east, and rivers to the north and west). They had it all.

By 1883 this fire company started changing. Stoker William Watkins was promoted to Engineer; however, the company Foreman was out of reach and was not realized until 1923. Chicago personnel records indicate William Watkins was hired in March of 1872, perhaps making him the first to be hired, and later to be assigned to Engine 21.

Stoker William Watkins

By 1888, Engine 21 was in the news again, as purported by the *Chicago Tribune:*

*A runaway team of horses carrying a small boy flew past quarters and a member of Engine 21 was said to have leaped into the wagon, rescuing the small boy, cart and horse.*

The heroic firefighter was never named, stealing the thunder of his act. This type of publicity of heroism helped build the Chicago Fire Department's image of courage in the face of danger, thereby maintaining and solidifying the image of Black Firefighters as heroes.

Regardless of Engine Company 21's accomplishments, integrating and participating in the Fireman's Benevolent Associations was questioned during this same period. The purpose of the association was to provide resources for the relief of distressed, sick, injured and disabled members, and to support the families of firefighters killed in the line of duty. The organization's by-laws stipulated that each company elected a member to the board of directors. Black men from Engine 21 were explicitly barred from this organization.

Bailey stated, "By banning these men, White firefighters rejected any Implications of brotherhood with Black Firefighters and their perceived inferiority."

By 1884, firefighter Wilson C. Hawkins who was finally admitted as a representative suggested racial boundaries in the department social sphere were permeable to a certain degree, as stated by Bailey.

Public opinion still played a role in white society's acceptance of Engine 21 as a group of Black firefighters. A former white volunteer firefighter named FA Bragg dismissed Engine 21 as inferior. He further alleged that the Black members of Engine 21 kept experienced white volunteer firefighters from joining the reorganized department. Furthermore, he claimed that colored firefighters endangered the lives and property of fellow white firefighters and the public with their unacceptable ignorance. Bragg felt that Blacks were only qualified to work as coach drivers and horsemen - jobs that required little skill or technical knowledge. In response to Bragg's demeaning comments, a former Engineer, Isaiah Washington wholeheartedly disagreed. He felt that Engine 21 always provided faithful and reliable service.

In 1885, a three-alarm fire in a Chicago lumber yard jumped the Chicago River and much of the South Side's neighboring town of Lake. Seventeen fire companies attempted, but failed, to contain the blaze. Engine 21's members went within ten feet of the burning lumber pile and soon made an impression on the flames. In helping to contain this blaze and risking their own lives, this fire company showcased their skills and worth as members of the department. The Chicago Fire Department annual report for 1893 stated:

*Engine 21 traveled more miles than any other company, responded to 474 alarms (compared to 360), worked 184 hours (compared to 110), and performed duties at 148 alarms (compared to 75). Engine 21 met and exceeded the expectations many White Chicagoans placed on them.*

Former Cook County Commissioner John Jones stated, "Engine 21's ten men did the work of normally 15."

Engine 21 was constantly challenged concerning their competence to serve. The Images of dark town and racist comments by former white firefighters reflected the fears that Blacks were not suited for positions that required non-agricultural skills, particularly an occupation like firefighting where incompetence could result in the deaths of innocent people or company members. It was not until 1943 that Chicago received its second Black fire company: Engine 16. Engine 16 was organized 71 years later.

At the turn of the century, Black Chicagoans were being left out and excluded from being hired and promoted. In 1889, the city rejected cries from the Black public to appoint a Black Fire Captain. Local Blacks petitioned Mayor Washburne and the city's Fire Commissioner demanding he appoint a Black Fire Captain which was denied.

# SEVEN

## PHOTOS TO DEPICT THE CHALLENGES AND CHANGES OF CHICAGO'S BLACK COMMUNITY

An example of Chicago's housing stock when most homes and apartments were built of wood, sidewalks, light poles and a cord of wood off to the right in the photo. This photo shows how hard firefighters worked to keep this fire from spreading. *Newberry library collection*.

19<sup>th</sup> century – WC Ellington Engineer for engine 21 at a working fire.

Engine Company 21 operating at an extra-alarm fire. Corner of Canal/VamBuren Street. Notice the high fire hydrant. Street grade levels were later raised to the current height they are today. *Information taken from Ken Little/John McNalis. Volume 1 History of Chicago Fire Houses of the 19<sup>th</sup> Century.*

Chicago's 1919 Race riots, blacks who lived outside of the selected black community were forced to relocate because of threats of violence and bombings.

A white mob attacked a black man and pulled him off the bus in Chicago as violence escalates.*Vivian G. Harsh collection-CPL*

A black family relocating after more threats of violence by a gang of white thugs who threw bricks and bombed homes where blacks lived. *Vivian G. Harsh collection-CPL*

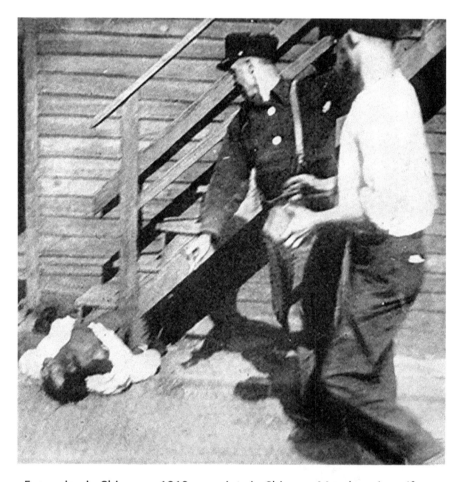

Expansion in Chicago – 1919 race riots in Chicago. Members in uniform appear to be firefighters. When there were crimes against blacks, whites were almost never arrested; and no one served time for these and other crimes committed. *Vivian G. Harsh collection-CPL*

Expansion of the black community – 1919 race riots in Chicago
*Vivian G. Harsh collection-CPL*

Chicago's dilapidated and over-crowed housing stock early 1900.
*Chicago public library.*

# EIGHT

## THE 20ᵀᴴ CENTURY

20ᵗʰ Century – Captain Joseph Wickliffe

Fifty-one years later, in 1923, Joseph Wickliffe, former Kentuckian, was promoted to Captain. Institutional racism was flourishing with legal statutes established and maintained, and racial segregation in public schools was affecting social accommodations, including transportation and housing. Through these illustrations and laws, Black Chicagoans, including members of Engine 21, were marked as inferior and unworthy of citizenship, thus allowing Whites to exploit, coerce and dehumanize them without impunity. Blacks then decided that they would work and vote in a political block. They vowed they would only support politicians committed to securing a portion of the public patronage, which was to be distributed to every nationality.

The image of the Best Man was argued by Glenda Gilmore in her analysis of post-war North Carolina. The prevalent Best Man ideology held that only men who exhibited benevolence, fairmindedness, and gentility merited the rights of manhood, namely the right to vote and hold office. In denying Black men their American rights to manhood and the right to vote and hold office, whites blatantly violated the Fifteenth Amendment, a key component in the interracial democracy, which the state at one time hoped to establish. Blacks paid taxes but were denied legislative and congressional representation.

By 1907, Truck 17 burned a Negro firefighter in effigy, all to keep a Black man from being assigned to that fire house. Feelings against the presence of the Colored Man as a member of the fire company was so strong that the foreman said they would not sleep in the same dormitory with Blacks. Firefighter John Jackson (Engine 21 first Line of Duty Death member in 1928), newly hired firefighter was assigned to Truck 7; but he was forced to transfer after members of Truck 7 went on strike to keep segregated fire houses among firefighters. The Civil Service Commission refused to send a recruit at the top of the list to be assigned to Engine 21 and created a separate employment eligibility list - one Black and one White. The Chicago Fire Department and the Civil Service Commission signaled that Black firefighters would not be afforded equal status within the fire department, further stimulating unequal treatment.

# NINE

## EXPANSION OF CHICAGO'S
## BLACK COMMUNITY

A typical black family migrating from the south to cities in the north seeking better paying jobs, schools and living accommodations. Blacks took part in what became the great migration to northern cities during WWI when over 100,000 blacks migrated into Chicago between 1910 & 1920. - Vivian Harsh collection.

Migration of Blacks from the South, and the Europeans from Europe, caused Chicago's population to balloon and continue to grow by leaps and bounds. Its population grew from 500,000 people in 1880 to over 1.5 million by 1900. By 1910, Chicago's black community had grown to 44,000 Black residents with a total population of over 2 million people, but still only one fire company. By this time a second shift was added allowing its members one day of rest before returning to duty, taking the stress off from working day in and day out. During this time, segregation in the city was in full effect. Renting to Blacks was confined to the Black Belt and Bronzeville Communities, creating overcrowded living conditions, unsanitary health conditions and the creation of the kitchenette and basement apartments; further straining emergency services and public safety.

In March 1888, The Chicago Tribune reported, after an inspection of company quarters, Engine 21 had four horses - Hiram, Frank, Logan and Fred - but by 1921 modernization came to the department and horse-drawn carriages gave way to automobiles and trucks. In 1921, Engine 21 was assigned a Seagrave pumper, with a maximum GPM flowing of 1,000 GPM and a large hose bed. These new vehicles allowed for even faster response times from its members, allowing them to travel to fires in gas driven vehicles.

Complaints from Chicago's Black community never wavered, the Chicago Defender reported requests made for assigning a second fire company, possibly a Hook & Ladder Company to assist the engine company, to the promotion of a Black fire captain; and a request for building repair when the fire house on Taylor Street fell in disrepair, but all fell on deaf ears. Amber Bailey's contention of engine 21's experiment in democracy extended to integration.

From 1931 to 1936, Truck 11 maintained one shift Black and one White. By 1936, these members were returned to Engine 19's quarters because of segregation and the cities unwillingness to fully man two fire companies of Black firefighters. When they returned to engine 19 quarters they split their duties between Engine 19 and high-pressure rig #7 to augment the excess manpower. The only other times when integration was considered was in early 1900 - Deichan, a white candidate, was assigned to Engine 21 and was managed by white officers, which continued until 1923.

In 1919, Chicago experienced three days of riots, bombings, and mob violence following the stoning death of a Black youth who drowned at 29th Street Beach because he wandered on the white side of the beach. Chicago was breaking at the seams. Between 1915 and 1922, Chicago experienced what came to be known as the great migration, when 60 to 70,000 Black people moved to Chicago from the south seeking better paying jobs, better schools and better housing. However, Blacks did not receive any of their wishes. Segregation and discrimination in housing, jobs and social services produced a city within a city. The Black Belt, well-established, extended south on State Street from Roosevelt Road to 31st Street and extended two blocks east and west of State Street.

At that point, Bronzeville grew east of State Street, (22nd Street) and South Park Place to 35th Street east to Cottage Grove, extending south to 39th Street. Whites worked to confine blacks to these overcrowded areas and discouraged others. They also discouraged renters and realtors from renting or selling properties outside of these areas. When property was sold or rented to Blacks outside of these boundaries they became victims of intimidation from arson to bombings, both blacks and whites alike.

The University of Chicago published, "The Negro in Chicago, a study of race relations and riots identified over 150 bombings recorded in properties bought or rented by Blacks. Wealthy Black banker and realtor Jessie Binga, became a target of violence by a terrorist at his home and business five times. He lived in an all-white community located at 5922 South Park Blvd.

Firefighter Fred Morgan Sr. Assigned to Engine 19,
3444 S. Rhodes Avenue, abt. 1945, *Allen Williams photo collection*

With this chaos of arson fires, overcrowding, bombings, and riots, Engine 21's duties increased exceptionally. By April 1927, Engine 21 relocated to Engine 19's quarters, 3444 S. Rhodes, in the heart of Bronzeville, but shared fire duties with a White truck company, Truck 11 and Truck 15. By 1920, Chicago's Black community grew to more than 110,000 people among Chicago's total population of 2.5 million.

Acting Lieutenant John Jackson was Engine 19's, or, Engine 21's first Line of Duty Death member dated January 6, 1928. Engine 19 was involved in a traffic accident with Truck 11 at the intersection of 35th and Indiana Ave., with both rigs meeting at the intersection. Acting Lieutenant Jackson was thrown from the apparatus and pinned between both vehicles. The fire run was a false alarm (steam).

On February 30, 1936, another member of Engine 19, Firefighter Hodd Bond was the second Black LODD member. Firefighter Bond, driver of high-pressure rig #7 assigned to Engine19's quarters, left quarters later than usual responding to an alarm, but the rig wouldn't start. When he finally got the rig started, Bond crashed with the Battalion buggy at the corner of 35th and Cottage Grove Ave., where he was thrown from his apparatus and succumbed to a broken neck. His story and his family's story is a noble one.

Hodd the elest son born in Chicago. In 1894 fought in World War I in France. He was a member of the 93rd Division, 370th regiment. The 370th regiment was a combat unit and saw extensive action.

Hodd and my grandmother were very close although he was 14 years older than her. She adored him. They wrote each other continuously during the war. He returned from the war safely and later became a fireman at Engine Company 19. He was killed when a practical joker turned in a false alarm resulting in a collision at 35th and Cottage Grove with a chief's car causing Hodd to be thrown over the windshield and dying of a broken neck in 1936.

Hodd Bond, Chicago's second LODD member, 1936 was a WWI Veteran and whose family came to Chicago in 1866 from Vincennes, Indiana. His father, a retired police officer, was a Civil War Veteran and their family earned their freedom while serving during the revolutionary war. *Hodd Bond family collection.*

Firefighter Bond's family gained their freedom in America during the Revolutionary War when his great grandfather, a Black Slave, was promised his freedom for serving in the war. Their family has representatives in the following wars: Revolutionary War, Civil War, Spanish American War and World War I, leading up to Hodd Bond. He was shot in the leg and received an award from the French Government for his gallantry. His father, Enoch Bond, relocated to Chicago in 1866 following the war, where he eventually served as a Chicago Police Officer in the Englewood District in the 1880's and 1890's, thus, making his family one of the oldest Black families still living in Chicago today.

In 1890, the Chicago Tribune published a story of African Americans protesting and petitioning Chicago for equal rights in the city regarding jobs, housing and virtually the same rights they were granted during the reconstruction period in America. This experiment in democracy was put on hold as a nation for the sake of individual and States rights. During this period the negative effects of Jim Crow laws led to Blacks fighting for the civil rights that they were previously granted during reconstruction.

Black migration and expansion with more Black fire houses was extremely slow. In 1943, Engine 16 became the Black community's 2nd black fire company manned by seven or eight members per shift, adding to Black employment and eventually promotions. By 1943, Chicago's Black community was bulging at the seams. Tenement housing was at an all- time high and fire safety was constantly in question. Boarders were common, and single-family dwellings were cut up to accommodate three or more families per floor, making fire deaths common with 15 to 20 people per floor. In 1943, the Black population rose to approximately 277,700 residents and spread from the North, West and South Sides of the city, with a majority living in Bronzeville and the Black Belt.

Notable Black scholars and political scientists such as: James Winbush, second generation firefighter, attributes black success of employment as firefighters to periods of insurrection in Chicago, when Blacks decided to fight back. For instance, during the 1919 race riots in Chicago a Black woman's breast was cut off and placed on a street light pole at 47th Street and Wentworth Ave. Blacks sought revenge by meeting White people exiting trains at the 18th Street Station with clubs and shot guns.

In 1939, Mayor Kelly failed to hire additional Black police officers to protect the Black policy wheel from the mob's take over. In 1943, Mayor Kelly kept his promise to hire 50 Black police officers, when elected. Emmitt Till's death sparked the Civil Rights movement, resulting in the Civil Rights Act, Voting Rights Act and the Fair Housing Act between 1964 and 1968, granting blacks the same rights that were guaranteed during the Reconstruction Period, 1865-1877.

After Engine 21 changed fire house locations, these same members were now in the heart of the Black community, Bronzeville. By 1930, Chicago's Black community had ballooned to 233,000 Black residents with a total population of 3.7 million people. However, they needed more Black fire companies. During this period, it was said that before another Black firefighter was hired another would have to die, retire or be rendered disabled.

Other Black fire companies followed Engine 16: June 1944, Truck 11; May 1949, Engine 48; 1951, Engine 12; 1953, Engines 9 and 53; 1954, Engine 6; 1955, Engine 45 and Truck 15; and June 1956, Ambulance #4. During this increase of Black fire companies and Black employees, these companies were primarily manned by White officers. Due to segregation and discrimination, they had always limited promotions for Black men as firefighters in the fire service. It was rumored that White officers were detailed to Black fire houses as punishment for drinking or inability to perform.

In many instances the Black community had always been utilized as a training ground because of the frequency of fires. However, it took the city more than 50 years to assign a Black Fire Captain; over 70 years to assign a second Black fire company; and almost 100 years to get more Blacks promoted to the upper ranks.

It was not until 1967 when Chicago's black firefighters realized an increase in the promotions of company officers. The 1940's and 1950's appeared to be a time when America experienced an increase in other Northern and Southern cities as firefighters. As a result, it was not until WWI and WWII when America succumbed to hiring Black men nationally for manpower in cities like Macon, Savannah and Charleston during the early 1800's. Gordon Grandpre stated, "The only reason blacks were hired was because the fire department didn't pay much and there were better paying jobs available for veterans."

These wars alone caused a need for firefighter manpower nationally; but without that, employment of Black firefighters would not have been permitted. Without the reformist practices of Mayor Medill in 1872, following the first great fire, Chicago never would have acquired a full complement of men to manage a whole company of Black firefighters - never in a million years.

Heroism in the line of duty was common with Engine 21, Engine 19 and Truck 11. Engine 21 responded to most major fires of consequence in Chicago's downtown business district, including the Iroquois Theater fire in 1903. In 1910, Engine 21 was acknowledged for their work performed at the Stock Yards Fire when 21 firefighters were killed, including a Chief Officer.

Members of Truck 11 in front of quarters, early 1940's,
*CAAFFM photo collection*

Over the years, many brave Black firefighters received awards for heroism. In 1929, Captain Joseph Wickliffe of Engine 19 and its members: Arthur Jones, Emanuel Jones, Robert Hudson, Matthew Grier, Sidney Dawson, Richard Downing, John Burk, and Lewis Stewart all received merit awards for their heroic efforts. In 1932, Firefighter Grant Chaney and Vernon Carrington, both members of Truck 11 received merit awards for their heroic efforts. Firefighter Lee Walton of Truck 11 and Emmitt Robinson of Truck 15 were both Medal of Honor winners. It has been said that Engine 21 and Engine 19, as a fire company, received more awards than any other fire company in Chicago.

Change has always come about in Chicago following some unforeseen tragedy. Black firefighters were hired following the great Chicago Fire when there was a need for more manpower and because of the tenacity of a stubborn visionary, Mayor Medill. World War I and WWII caused a need for brave men to serve. Chicago 1919 race riots, and integration made its transition from segregation to integration in 1965 when a

Black woman, Dessie Mae Williams was struck and killed by a driveress Tillerman of Truck 26 on Chicago's Westside community. Violent riots followed along with looting and burning of Westside businesses. All resulted because of negligent hiring practices by the city, including their refusal to employ Black men as firefighters on the Westside, as well as the disrespect and excessive property damage by white firefighters. Some Westside residents explained they had never seen a Black Firefighter before and were unaware that Chicago had Black Firefighters.

The next day following a night of chaotic rage and fury, the Chicago Fire Department announced that Black Firefighters, night riders, would be detailed to these troubled areas of the Westside so Black people could see Black Firefighters at work in their communities. Two years following these riots President Lyndon Johnson appointed an 11-member board to investigate this race riot and concluded segregation and poverty have created in the racial ghetto a destructive environment totally unknown to most White Americans. Our nation has moved toward two societies: one Black and one White, separate and unequal. Black and White Firefighters have coexisted together ever since, but some seem to gravitate to more clandestine fire houses where many are familiar with one another.

# IN CONCLUSION

Today, America's experiment of inter-racial democracy as a test to America's will to live and work together toward the American dream has been few and far between for many Black people. Americans, in most cases, are reluctant in trusting the American Dream as it is written in our constitution *with equality for all*. An example would be the absence of big business in the Black Community, evident in 1872 and today. Riots, such as the 1921 race riot in Tulsa, Oklahoma, devastated a thriving black community that was self-reliant and independent. Institutional racism in America is at an all-time high and is still practiced regularly today. It is said, they would "rather pay you, rather than let you play".

Deputy Fire Marshall, Chief Grant Chaney, recognized as
Chicago's first Black Battalion Chief promoted 1958, *CFD photo collection*

The Chicago Fire Department's snail-like approach to hiring and promoting Blacks continues to plague the Black Community's vanguard in times of need, despite our contribution to its tax base. Another example is in 1956-58 when the first Black Battalion Chief, Mike Ellis, was promoted, 86 years following the hiring of the first Black Firefighter. Chief Grant Chaney allowed Mike Ellis to be first because of his age.

Finally, in 1958, Chief Chaney was promoted and was always given credit for being promoted as the first Black Battalion Chief. Chief Chaney spent his entire career as a member of Truck 11 before his promotion to Battalion Chief.

Chief Edwin Williams was third in line to be promoted to Chief. He then was promoted to First Deputy Division Marshall in 1963. In 1967, a large promotion took place for Blacks when it realized promotions from Engineer to Chief Officer.

Blacks have never been hired on the Chicago Fire Department in great numbers without the assistance of the courts and local Executive orders which forced the city to employ Black men and women as firefighters; i.e., In 1872 when Mayor Medill established Engine 21; in 1977 when Affirmative action was granted following a consent decree by the courts; and in 1980 when black strike breakers were hired for fear of busting the strike and to make up for past hiring practices.

I cannot, in good conscience, write about Engine 21 without discussing the events that led up to their existence to gain and maintain employment. Engine 21 was America's vanguard to its community and was the experiment in Democracy that allowed Blacks to serve in the fire service. Without this opportunity, Black people would still be on the outside looking in. These men proved that when given the opportunity they were just as competent and fully capable of preserving life and property.

# ABOUT THE AUTHOR

R etired Battalion Chief Dekalb E. Walcott Jr. served 31 years as a Chicago firefighter starting his career in November 1978 as a 30-day wonder and hired during affirmative action. Chicago Fire Department was short of personnel, as a result Fire Academy training only lasted 30 days.

Throughout his career Dekalb served as Firefighter to Battalion Chief along with serving in fire prevention and public education. He has received numerous awards for community service, served as Chairman for Black Firefighters day and was responsible for helping Chicago establish a smoke detector and carbon monoxide ordinance in the mid 1980's. Dekalb sponsored a 100-photo pictorial display during Black History month in February of 1984 honoring Chicago's unsung Black

Heroes of Fire, which started his career as Chicago's Black Firefighter historian.

Dekalb has served on the executive board of the African American Firefighters and Paramedic League of Chicago as historian, corresponding secretary, sergeant at arms, vice president and President. Today he spends his time researching black firefighter history and publishing its work. He is married to his wife of 34 years and has two sons: Dekalb is a 10-year firefighter and Matthew is a student with law school aspirations.

# THE CHICAGO AFRICAN AMERICAN FIREFIGHTERS MUSEUM

The Chicago African American Firefighters Museum (CAAFFM) grew out of a vision originally proposed by retired fireman Henry 'Hank' Webster, Lawrence Burns, and Morris Davis and adopted by the Ole Tymers organization all recognizing themselves as part of a proud but unsung tradition of Black Firefighters, these men envisioned an institution that would honor and pay tribute to the legacy of African Americans in the Fire service. With that in mind, CAAFFM was founded in 2007.

In March 2013, CAAFFM moved into its present location at 5349 S. Wabash Avenue, in the former fire house of Engine Company 61 and Ambulance 36, which had served the surrounding community since

1928. Today CAAFFM is interested in renovating this historic Chicago landmark into a world class museum whose mission is to collect, exhibit and conserve artifacts, photographs, documents and stories that convey the rich history of African American Firefighters.

Chicago holds a distinguished place within this history. In December 1872, the Chicago Fire Department Engine Company 21 became the first paid professional Black Firefighting company in the United States. In addition to blazing the trail for future generations of Black Firefighters, this pioneering company made an indelible mark in the history of firefighting when they invented the sliding pole, which became an iconic fixture in firehouses throughout the United States. Stories such as these abound in the rich history of African American Firefighters, as Black Firefighters, men and women throughout the nation carved out an enduring legacy of triumph, innovation and valor.

All profits from this book go towards CAAFFM organization.

# CHICAGO'S FIRST CITIZEN IN THE 1790'S

Photo of John Baptist Point Du sable.
Credits to Chicago public library

The first permanent settler in Chicago was a black man named Jean Baptiste Point DuSable. He was born on the island of Haiti around 1745 to a French mariner and a mother who was a slave of African descent.

DuSable was educated in France and then, in the early 1770s, sailed to New Orleans. From there, he made his way up the Mississippi River to Peoria, Illinois where he married a Potawatomi woman named Catherine in a tribal ceremony. The couple had two children, Jean

Baptiste Point DuSable, Jr. and Suzanne. The marriage formally recognized before a Catholic priest in Cahokia, Illinois in 1778.

DuSable settled along the northern bank of the Chicago River near Lake Michigan ca. 1779 and developed a prosperous trading post and farm.

At his trading post, DuSable served Native Americans, British, and French explorers. He spoke Spanish, French, English, and several Native American dialects, which served him well as an entrepreneur and mediator.

DuSable sold his estate on May 7, 1800 and returned to Peoria, Illinois. He later moved to St. Charles, Missouri, where he died on August 28, 1818.

# CHICAGO'S GREAT BLACK HEROES OF FIRE
# 101 YEARS, 1872 – 1973

**(Less than 300 black members hired in 100 years)**

1. James E. Porter-1st Black assistant Foreman/Lt.
2. Willie Hawkins
3. James Johnson
4. Stephine Paine
5. George Adams
6. George Reed-member who slid the first sliding pole
7. William Watkins-First Black Engineer 1883

**Members who served following the first seven members**

8. Edward Adams
9. Edmond Adams
10. Robert Allen
11. Maynard Alleyne
12. Robert Ambrose
13. Nathaniel Anderson
14. Clifford Armstead
15. Arthur Bacon
16. James Banks
17. Walter Banks
18. Charles Bailey
19. William Bates
20. Johnny Barnes
21. Richard Barryman
22. Leroy Belt
23. Joe Boatner
24. Leemon Boatner
25. William Boyer

26.  Leroy Bolden
27.  Hodd Bond-2nd lodd member
28.  Martin Boarman
29.  Bishop Boyd
30.  Jim Brooks
31.  Clarence Brown
32.  Collins Brown Sr.
33.  Earl Brown
34.  Henry Brown
35.  Dudley Broadnax
36.  Charles Bronaugh
37.  Chalmus Bronaugh
38.  Eugene Broughton
39.  Ulysses Brunson
40.  Lawrence Burns
41.  Wendell Burrell
42.  James Burke
43.  Earnest Cade
44.  Richard Caesar
45.  William Cartwright
46.  Wilbur Carridine
47.  Roy Carroll
48.  Julius Carey
49.  Richard Caesar
50.  Archie Chaney
51.  Grant Chaney-recognized as Chicago's first Black Battalion Chief
52.  Arthur Charleston Sr.
53.  Arthur (Blue)Charleston Jr.
54.  Edward Chestnut
55.  James E. Chestnut
56.  Edmond Clark
57.  Joseph Claybon
58.  Frank Cochran
59.  James Coggins

60. Boise Coleman
61. Clarence Collins
62. Leonard Coper
63. William Coppedge
64. Julius Cowan
65. Frank Cochran
66. James Cook Jr.
67. Julius Cowan
68. Joseph Craft
69. Bennie Crane
70. James Cross
71. Johnny Crutcher
72. Newton Curry
73. Thomas Daniels
74. Walter Davenport
75. Morris Davis
76. Sidney Dawson
77. Victor De Coudreaux
78. Franscio De La Cerna
79. Houston Diemer
80. Richard Downing
81. James Dudley
82. Lamar Duke
83. Miller Duncan
84. James Echols
85. Andrew Lefty Edwards
86. David Edwards
87. Earnest Edwards
88. Tim Edwards
89. Sam Eggleston
90. Leland Elder
91. Mike Ellis
92. CW (buster) Ellington
93. Russell Ellington
94. WC Ellington

95.  William Elligan
96.  Mike Ellis
97.  Clarence Ellison
98.  George Evans
99.  James Everly
100.  Russ Ewing
101.  David Ferguson
102.  James Finney
103.  McKinley Fleming
104.  David Flournoy
105.  Charles Gamble
106.  John Gardner
107.  Carl Garnes
108.  Charles Gault
109.  Robert Gay
110.  Ralph Glover
111.  William Gordon
112.  Gordan Grand pre
113.  Maurice Gravitt
114.  Will Gray
115.  William Green
116.  Matthew Grier
117.  Ben Griffin
118.  Robert Bob Griger
119.  Clarence Hall
120.  Charles Hampton
121.  Theodore Hansen
122.  Carl Harris
123.  Clearley Harris
124.  Dave Harris
125.  James Hasty
126.  James Harris
127.  Rusty Henderson
128.  Tom Henderson
129.  Wayne Henderson

130. William Herron
131. Roger Hill
132. William Hillbring
133. Thomas Hodges
134. Cortez Holland
135. William Horton
136. Willie Horton
137. Robert Hudson
138. Joe Hurlon
139. Theodore Ted Ingram
140. Grant Jackson
141. Hugh Jackson
142. John Jackson
143. Larry Jackson
144. Spencer Jackson
145. Charley Johnson
146. Donald Johnson
147. Larney Johnson
148. Ralph Johnson
149. Alonzo Jones
150. Charles Jones
151. George Jones
152. Robert Jordan
153. Cyrus Joyner
154. James Kennebrew
155. James Kilcrease
156. Wesley Knox
157. Russell Lewis
158. Oswald Lewis
159. William Lofton
160. Newton Long
161. Buddy Lyle
162. Anthony Makin
163. Charles Matthews
164. David Mayberry

165. Landis McAlpine
166. Bernard McCray
167. Woody McCune
168. Carl McFerren
169. Mitchell McGuire
170. George Meeks
171. Thessaloni Montegan
172. Carlise Moore
173. Cloyd Moran
174. Bud Moran
175. Fred Morgan Sr.
176. Fred Morgan Jr.
177. Stanford Murry
178. Jasper Neal
179. Harry Nesbit
180. Curry Newton
181. Les Outerbridge
182. Louis Palmer
183. Paul Pamon
184. Thomas Parker
185. Johnny Parker
186. Elwain Parks
187. Edward Partee
188. Charles Pickett
189. Floyd President
190. Benjamin Ramsey
191. Joe Reese
192. Rick Reynolds-created Chicago fire department calendar
193. Perry Roberts
194. Arthur Robbie Robinson
195. Emmit Robinson
196. Nathaniel Robinson Jr.
197. Raymond Robinson
198. Theodore Robinson
199. Myron Ross

200. Edward Sayers
201. James Sawyer
202. Andre Scott
203. Andrew Scott
204. Charles Scott
205. Jerome Scott
206. Jim Slyer
207. Charles Smeltzer
208. Crawford Smith
209. Don Smith
210. Harry Smith
211. Norman Smith
212. Norman Smith
213. Robert Smith
214. Warren Smith
215. Loyal Spitzer
216. Beverly Southernland
217. Edward Steed
218. Charles Stewart
219. Edmond Stewart
220. Jessie Stewart
221. Lawrence Stewart
222. John Street
223. Edward Stokes
224. Sidney Stover
225. Thomas Supthon
226. John Sublette
227. Eugene Suggs
228. Harry Sunbart
229. Howard Sykes
230. Sherman Tarver
231. Frank Thomas
232. Gaylord Thomas
233. Fletcher Thompson
234. Robert Lucious Thompson

235. Westly Thompson
236. Cleophus Trimm
237. Leslie Turner
238. Melvin Turner
239. Percy Turner
240. Dodo Walker
241. Dennis Walters
242. Lee Walton
243. Marshall Ward
244. Ado Warren
245. Ira Washington
246. WE Matthews
247. Henry Webster
248. Kenneth Westbrook
249. Charles White
250. Joseph Wickliffe-First Black civil service Lieutenant & Captain
251. John Wicks
252. George Wilkes
253. Allen Williams
254. Cleo Williams
255. Edwin Williams
256. Hubert Williams
257. Leroy Williams
258. Maurice Williams
259. Richard (Rick) Williams
260. Sylvester Williams
261. Bob Willis
262. James Winbush Sr.
263. James Winbush Jr.
264. Steve Winbush
265. Albert Wilson
266. Tommy Woolfolk
267. Roscoe Woosley
268. Frank Wright

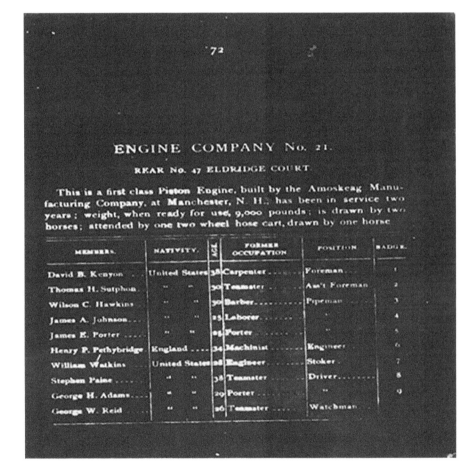

72

## ENGINE COMPANY No. 21.

### REAR No. 47 ELDRIDGE COURT

This is a first class Piston Engine, built by the Amoskeag Manufacturing Company, at Manchester, N. H., has been in service two years; weight, when ready for use, 9,000 pounds; is drawn by two horses; attended by one two wheel hose cart, drawn by one horse

| MEMBERS. | NATIVITY. | AGE | FORMER OCCUPATION | POSITION | BADGE. |
|---|---|---|---|---|---|
| David B. Kenyon | United States | 38 | Carpenter | Foreman | 1 |
| Thomas H. Sutphon | " " | 30 | Teamster | Ass't Foreman | 2 |
| Wilson C. Hawkins | " " | 30 | Barber | Pipeman | 3 |
| James A. Johnson | " " | 25 | Laborer | " | 4 |
| James E. Porter | " " | 25 | Porter | " | 5 |
| Henry P. Pethybridge | England | 34 | Machinist | Engineer | 6 |
| William Watkins | United States | 28 | Engineer | Stoker | 7 |
| Stephen Paine | " " | 38 | Teamster | Driver | 8 |
| George H. Adams | " " | 29 | Porter | " | 9 |
| George W. Reid | " " | 36 | Teamster | Watchman | |

# SPECIAL ACKNOWLEDGEMENTS

*A special acknowledgement goes out to those neglected Chicago Firefighters whose story never would have been told without this publication. "Greater love hath no man than this that a man lay down his life for his friends". (John 15:13) These men are true heroes of fire.*

## Chicago Black Noble Line of Duty Death (LODD) members

- January 6th, 1928 – Acting Lt. John Jackson of Engine 19, involved in a traffic accident with Truck 11, corner of 35th & Indiana, while responding to an alarm.
  http://thechicagocitizen.com/news/2015/aug/19/fallen-black-firefighters-honored-chatham-neighbor/

- February 30th, 1936 – Firefighter Hodd Bond of Engine 19, apparatus involved in a collision with battalion buggy while responding to an alarm, intersection of 35th & Cottage Grove. *Death 30 May 1936
  https://search.ancestry.com/collections/2542/records/2805031/printer-friendly?tid=53407305&pid=132031745860&usePUB=true&_phsrc=WRO2570&_phstart=successSource

- November 12th, 1973 – EMT Jessie Edwards of Ambulance 38 struck by a car at 63rd & Woodlawn Ave. bystander and patient were killed.
  https://www.fsi.illinois.edu/content/library/IFLODD/search/firefighter_detail.cfm?ff_id=97

On November 12, 1973, Jesse Edwards, a civilian paramedic serving on a Chicago Fire Department ambulance, died in the line of duty when he was struck by a vehicle driven by a drunk driver. The ambulance had responded to an alarm for a woman who had collapsed from chest pains, and Edwards and the other paramedics had just placed the woman in the back of the ambulance when the drunk driver crashed into them. Edwards suffered severe injuries and was transported to Billings Hospital where he died during surgery.

**Citations:** James Elsner and Joe Monrang, "Car rams crowd behind ambulance; 1 dies, 6 hurt," *Chicago Tribune*, November 13, 1973.

- August 9th, 1983 – Firefighter Sidney Brown, badge #1190, of Engine 75, trapped while attempting rescue at 122nd & State Street. (Park in Chicago named in 2015 in his honor. https://www.dnainfo.com/chicago/20150803/chatham/park-honoring-1st-black-fireman-die-line-of-duty-be-rededicated/ https://www.firehero.org/fallen-firefighter/sidney-brown/

- February 1st, 1985 – Firefighter Michael Talley, badge #3201, of Truck 58, roof collapse at 3-11 alarm fire at Vic Star Electronics store, 2847 N. Milwaukee Ave. https://www.firehero.org/?s=Michael+Talley

  http://articles.chicagotribune.com/1986-04-08/news/8601250670_1_exclusionary-rule-confession-strayhorn

  http://articles.chicagotribune.com/1986-11-23/news/8603270937_1_roof-rolling-firefighter

- July 4th, 1987 – Firefighter James Hill, badge #3330, of Truck 33, caught in a flash over in an attic, 4306 S. Wood Street. *Death 5 July 1987 age 44

  http://articles.chicagotribune.com/1987-07-06/news/8702190199_1_three-other-firefighters-smoke-inhalation-firefighters-injuries

  https://search.ancestry.com/cgi-bin/sse.dll?indiv=1&dbid=1501&h=3422050&tid=83427959&pid=272029734855&usePUB=true&_phsrc=WRO2587&_phstart=successSource

- December 22nd, 1989 – Firefighter Kelvin Anderson, badge #3753, of Engine 107, roof collapse at 3-11 alarm fire at Rose Sharon Church, 2950 W. Harrison Street. * Death 23 Dec. 1989 b. 11 Sept. 1962 https://search.ancestry.com/cgi-bin/sse.dll?indiv=1&dbid=1501&h=3520947&tid=83427959&pid=272029732545&usePUB=true&_phsrc=WRO2580&_phstart=successSource

- December 2nd, 1997, Assistant Deputy Fire Commissioner Jessie Stewart from Headquarters, involved in a car accident responding to a 2-11 alarm at 2447 W. North Ave. February 3rd, 1985. * Death 1 Dec. 1997

  https://search.ancestry.com/cgi-bin/sse.dll?indiv=1&dbid=3693&h=60050648&ssrc=pt&tid=83427959&pid=272029733656&usePUB=true

  Jesse Stewart died at the age of 73, in the line of duty. He was the Assistant Deputy Fire Commissioner. He had been critically injured in Feb 3, 1985 in a car accident while responding to an incident.

- February 12<sup>th</sup>, 1998 – Firefighter Anthony Lockhart, badge #2579, of Engine 120, caught in a flashover fire at 10611 S. Western Ave.

  https://www.fsi.illinois.edu/content/library/IFLODD/search/Image.cfm?ID=905&ff_id=213

- May 19<sup>th</sup>, 1998 – Firefighter Eugene Blackmon, badge #4008, a member of Squad #5, drowned during rescue operation – 135<sup>th</sup> & Indiana Ave. Calumet River.

  https://www.firehero.org/fallen-firefighter/eugene-w-blackmon-jr/

- April 29<sup>th</sup>, 2000 – Lieutenant L.C. Merrell, badge #520, of Truck 24, thrown from his apparatus after being struck by civilian truck at 107<sup>th</sup> & Throop Street. https://www.firehero.org/fallen-firefighter/l-c-merrell-jr/

- December 22<sup>nd</sup>, 2010 – Firefighter Corey Ankum, badge #6057, of Tower Ladder 34, Roof collapse at 3-11 alarm fire, 1744 E. 75<sup>th</sup> Street.

  https://www.dnainfo.com/chicago/20140515/south-shore-above-79th/building-owner-gets-jail-time-for-blaze-that-killed-two-firefighters/

  https://www.firehero.org/fallen-firefighter/corey-d-ankum/

- November 11<sup>th</sup>, 2012 – Firefighter Walter Patmon Jr., badge #2206, of Truck 40, chest pains in quarters after returning from fire, 1520 W. 99<sup>th</sup> Street. Died at Little Company of Mary Hospital.

  https://www.firehero.org/fallen-firefighter/walter-patmon-jr/

- Date – Firefighter died from chest pains following a fire.

# APPENDIX

# BIBLIOGRAPHY

1. A Biography of Chicago by Dominic A. Pacyga, Chicago

2. An Autobiography of Black Politics – Dempsy Travis, Real Estate covenants in Chicago

3. Ancestry.com; Federal census & civil war records

4. Chicago Daily Tribune Archives, March 1988 – The boys of Engine 21, ProQuest historical newspapers

5. Chicago Defender News, January 7th, 1928, John Jackson 1st Black firefighter LODD

6. Chicago Fire Department – LODD

7. Chicago historical society

8. Chicago Public Library – Vivian G. Harsh collection, Newberry library and Harold Washington library-city of Chicago Personnel division, Chicago Fire Department Annual Reports

9. Christopher Reed – Author/Retired History professor Roosevelt University, publisher of Black Chicago 1833-1900

10. Engine 21; An experiment with interracial democracy in an era of reconstruction by Amber Baily, published 2011

11. Fatal Fire truck accident sparked riot in 1965, by Linda Gartz, Chicago Defender News, August 18, 2015

12. Men of Colour, Race, riots and Black Firefighters struggle for equality from the AFA to the Valiants by John C. Mc Williams

13. Profiles of Courage, The rich history of African American Firefighters by Mike Legeros

14. Race & Firefighting in Antebellum south, history, published 2009 by Lykee B. Davis

15. The Encyclopedia of Chicago, by Grossman, Keating Reiff, U of C press, Oct. 2004

16. The History of Chicago Fire Houses of the 19th Century, volumes I, II & III, by Ken Little and John Mc Nalis

17. The Negro in Chicago, A study of race relations and riots, by The Chicago commission on Race Relations, published in 1922 by the University of Chicago press

18. The political History of Chicago, 1837-1887 by M.L. Ahern

19. Underground railroad in Illinois by Glennette Tilly Turner, January 2001

# PHOTO CREDITS

1. Cover photo contributed by Fredrick Olney, photo of the original members of Engine 21

2.  Rear photo & inside photo pg.2 by David Banks, Black Heroes of Fire logo

3. Pg. 9 – Engine 21 Allen Williams collection

4. Pg.10 – Unknown Firefighters-History of Black FF's-slaves/freedman-1850's j. paul getty museum & Robert W. Woodruff

5. Pg. 12 - Engine 21 racing to a fire up Wabash Ave. Allen Williams collection

6. Pg. 13 – 19$^{th}$ century Darktown fire brigade by currier and ives, published 1885-1890

7. Pg. 14 – Engine 21 uniform inspection-Allen Williams collection

8. Pg. 15 – Fredrick Olney, David Kenyon great grandson family photo collection, E-21 photo of original members

9. Pg. 16. Mayor Joseph Medill – Newberry Library photo collection

10. Pg. 17. John Jones – 1$^{st}$ Black Cook County Commissioner-Chicago Historical Society

11. Pg. 19. Chicago rubble from the first great fire of Oct. 1871-Newberry library photo collection

12. Pg. 20. Chicago housing stock – Newberry Library photo collection

13. Pg. 21. Maps of area burned in the fire of 1871 and black fire of July 1874, Chicago – A Biography of Chicago

14. Pg. 23. 1887 display of the Fire Pole – The political history of Chicago 1837-1887 M.L. Ahern

15. Pg. 24. David Kenyon – Newberry Library

16. Pg. 25. E-19 in front quarters 1930 – Bond family collection

17. Pg. 26. Engr. William Watkins -Chicago Historical society

18. Pg. 28. Chicago use of wood for homes and most things – Newberry library

19. Pg. 29. Engr. WC Ellington, Allen Williams photo collection

20. Pg. 29. Engine 21 at a working fire, corner of Canal & Van Buren, Ken Little photo collection

21. Pg.30. Photos of 1919 race riots Chicago, Vivian G. Harsh collection-cpl

22. Pg. 31. 1919 Race riots, FF with a brick, Vivian Harsh collection

23. Pg. 32. Photo of rundown tenant homes Chicago-Newberry library collection

24. Pg. 33. Captain Joseph Wickliffe – Allen Williams collection

25. Pg. 35. Typical black sharecropper family relocating from the south-Vivian Harsh Collection

26. Pg. 37. FF Fred Morgan in front of E-19's quarters – Allen Williams collection

27. Pg. 38. Hodd Bond 2nd black firefighter LODD, Hodd Bond family photo collection

28. Pg. 40. Truck 11 abt. 1945 – CAAFFM photo

29. Pg. 42. Battalion Chief Grant Chaney – Grant Chaney Family collection

30. Pg. 46. Jean Baptist Point Du Sable-Chicago's first citizen-Chicago Historical Society

31. Pg. 54. Engine 21''s company roster 1875 – CFD personnel records Harold Washington Library

# NOTES

1.  Lykee B. Davis, Race & Firefighting in Antebellum South, published 2009, pg. 2-5

2.  Amber Bailey, Engine 21 - An Experiment with Interracial Democracy in An Era of Reconstruction, 1872-1927, pg. 7-10

3.  Amber Bailey, Engine 21, pg. 15, 16

4.  Harold Washington Library, Chicago Fire Department Annual Report and Personnel Record, 1875,isted pg 73 (co. Roster. 1893 pg 31 run out times)

5.  Chicago Tribune Newspaper, 1888 - pg. 25,29 & 31

6.  Chicago Tribune Newspaper, Black Fire July 14, 1874 - pg 20, 21 & 22

7.  Ken Little & John McNalis, Volume I, II, III, The History of Chicago Fire Houses, pg. 24

8.  Chicago Commission on Race Relations, Negro, Race & Riots, 1922, U of C Press, pg. 46

9.  Chicago Fire Department LODD members, pg. 75-78

# WORKS CITED

Iroquois Theater Fire in Chicago – December 30, 1903
http://www.chicagotribune.com/news/nationworld/politics/chi
-chicagodays-iroquoisfire-story-story.html
http://explore.chicagocollections.org/image/chicagohistory/71
/3r0q087/

Chicago Mayor Joseph Medill (1823-1899)
http://www.chicagotribune.com/news/nationworld/politics/chi
-chicagodays-medill-story-story.html
https://en.wikipedia.org/wiki/Joseph_Medill

Joseph Kenyon (1838-1905) – Chicago Fire Department Chief

Chicago1880 Census report noting David Kenyon born in State of
New York
https://www.ancestry.com/interactive/6742/4240461-
00561?pid=46457951&backurl=https://search.ancestry.com/c
gi-
bin/sse.dll?indiv%3D1%26dbid%3D6742%26h%3D4645795
1%26tid%3D%26pid%3D%26usePUB%3Dtrue%26_phsrc%
3DWRO2566%26_phstart%3DsuccessSource&treeid=&pers
onid=&hintid=&usePUB=true&_phsrc=WRO2566&_phstart
=successSource&usePUBJs=true

Firefighters and Emergency Personnel Line of Duty Deaths
https://www.firehouse.com/lodds

Chicago African American Firefighters Museum Phone, (773) 262-
3210 · Address. 5349 S Wabash Av. Chicago, Illinois 60615

Facebook:  https://www.facebook.com/pages/Chicago-African-American-Firefighter-Museum/124137140974711

Website:  http://chicagoareafire.com/blog/2015/06/chicago-african-american-firefighters-museum/

Media:
https://www.dnainfo.com/chicago/20130326/bronzeville/first-black-firefighters-museum-clears-hurdle/

http://yourblackworld.net/2013/03/27/chicago-relocates-african-american-firefighter-museum-racially-divisive-firehouse-no-good/

Book Cited:  Dennis Smiths History of Firefighting in America
https://www.abebooks.com/9780803725386/Dennis-Smiths-History-Firefighting-America-0803725388/plp

## SPONSORS

Mella'Ninn Complex™☐ is grateful to be a small part in sponsorship for this knowledgeable book. As a small Black Owned Chicago Business, we are thrilled to network with community leaders such as the Author, Dekalb Walcott Jr., and other local businesses to further educate, create jobs and give revenue back to our neighborhoods. For more about how we got started visit us @ www.mellaninncomplex.com / Deirdre Monique, CEO/Product Developer

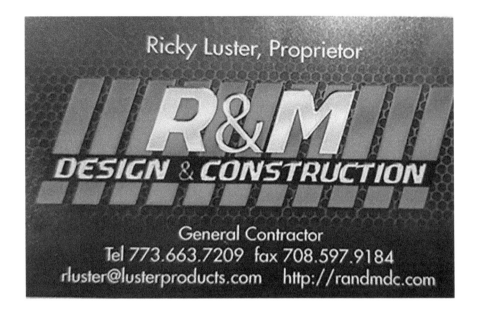

We at R & M Construction are proud sponsors of Black Heroes of Fire the untold history of Chicago's first Black Fire company. As a general contractor we provide full service remodeling design and construction. Whole house remodeling from basements to kitchens and baths. Licensed and bonded contractor.